THIS BOOK BELONGS TO:

With thanks to Kristin, for your advice on health and movement — S.R.

Adapted from:
See How We Move!: A First Book of Health and Well-Being

Text and illustrations © 2018 Scot Ritchie
All rights reserved.
Printed in China. THH

This special edition has been
printed for McDonald's Restaurants of Canada Limited.

The health and well-being recommendations in this book are provided
by the author, and should not be considered an official position
or recommendation of McDonald's Restaurants of Canada Limited.

Produced and published by Kids Can Press Ltd.,
25 Dockside Drive, Toronto, ON M5A 0B5

www.kidscanpress.com

The Golden Arches Design, McDonald's,
Happy Meal, Happy Meal Box Design,
House & Design and RMHC are trademarks of
McDonald's Corporation and its affiliates, licensed
to McDonald's Restaurants of Canada Limited.
©2021 McDonald's

See How We Move!
A First Book of Health and Well-Being

Scot Ritchie

Kids Can Press

Contents

Meet the Friends!

Come along with the five friends as they
get ready for their school's swim meet!
As the children prepare for the competition,
they discover that keeping their bodies
and minds healthy can enhance their
performance and improve their lives.
Join the friends and dive in!

Yulee

Martin

Sally

Nick

Pedro

Max

Ollie

Body and Mind

Tomorrow is a big day for our five friends. Their swim team, the Flying Sharks, is competing in the school meet. They've been preparing for weeks, training their bodies and minds in order to swim their best. Today, Nick's mom is taking everyone to the neighbourhood pool for one last practice. Then they will visit the community centre for a special surprise.

Do you ever think about how your body and mind work together? It's amazing what you can do if you put your mind to it!

Nick's House

Yulee's
Apartment
Building

Neighbourhood
Pool

Community Centre

Ready to Go!

"Does everyone have their goggles?" Nick's mom asks, as they're leaving for the pool.

Oh, no! Martin realizes he left his goggles at home. They help him to see clearly underwater, so he's happy to borrow an extra pair from Nick.

Yulee arrives on her bike — just in time! She's wearing her helmet to protect her head.

Using the proper equipment for your sport helps improve your performance — and it can also keep you safe. Yulee's helmet is sized to fit snugly so that it doesn't slip off if she has a fall.

Just Move!

On the way to the pool, the kids talk about sports and games they like to play. They know how important it is to get their bodies moving. Exercise helps your heart, lungs and muscles stay strong and healthy. It can also improve your mood and boost your energy level.

How do you get your body moving?

Activities that use your mind as much as your body are lots of fun. When you dance, you have to remember all the steps while moving quickly. That's called thinking on your feet!

You're Getting Warm

Before jumping in the pool, Coach Penny asks the kids to do warm-up exercises and some light stretching. Gently working your muscles before being active can help prevent injury. Martin and Yulee missed the last practice, so they are doing some extra warm-ups.

4 ... 5 ... 6 ...

Your body reacts in different ways when your muscles are working hard. You might breathe heavy and feel your heart beat faster. You can also sweat, get thirsty — or just feel great!

Jump In!

It's time to swim. Pedro starts the team off with their favourite stroke — the front crawl. Coach Penny looks at the clock.

"Ready, set, go!"

Everybody swims their best. Go, Flying Sharks!

Sally is disappointed that she came in last. But it helped a lot when she heard her teammates cheering her on.

I Can Do That!

After the race, Sally worries that she will let the team down at tomorrow's meet. She knows she can do better.

"I have good reach with my arms, but I need to kick harder," says Sally. "Then I'll go faster!"

"Good idea!" says Pedro. "Improving my kick really helped me."

Coach Penny helps when the team needs it. But it's also good for Sally to figure out solutions herself by understanding what she's good at and where she can improve.

It's Playtime!

That was a hard practice! Everybody is tired, but the Flying Sharks always finish with some stretching and a free swim to cool down. It's time to play!

When the ball hits the water, all of a sudden the five friends get a second wind! Finding a sport or activity to enjoy with friends is a great way to make sure you take part and stay active.

The friends always have fun during free swim. Keeping your body active and feeling good will help your mind feel good, too!

Team Huddle

After drying off, everybody is ready for snack time. But Pedro isn't hungry. He's nervous about tomorrow. Yulee knows what always makes her feel better, so she gathers the team together for a group hug!

There are things you can do if you feel anxious or sad. Talking to your teacher or parents, taking deep breaths and having quiet time can help you feel better. And you can help your friends feel better, too!

Wash Up!

No one on the team wants to get sick before the big meet! So the friends have been washing their hands regularly with soap and water. Handwashing helps to stop the spread of bad germs that can make you sick.

Germs are so tiny that you can only see them with a microscope. Coughing into your elbow and staying away from others when you're sick — or when *they* are — are two other ways to help bad germs from spreading.

Time to Refuel

Now everybody is hungry! After using up all that energy in the pool, the kids need fuel to keep their minds and bodies working well. Eating a variety of healthy foods and drinking lots of water will help you feel, and think, your best.

Eating a wide range of healthy foods is one of the best things you can do for your body. What are your favourite foods?

Body and Brain

Everybody looks the same on the inside. We all have bones, muscles, organs and a whole lot more! In this picture, can you see where your brain is, or the muscles in your legs? While you sleep, your body is working, digesting last night's dinner or repairing a bruised muscle. And your mind is working through problems and processing the day's events. Our bodies are amazing!

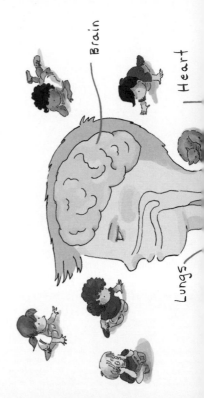

Nick's shoulder is sore from practice. He hopes it will feel better after a little more stretching and a good night's sleep.

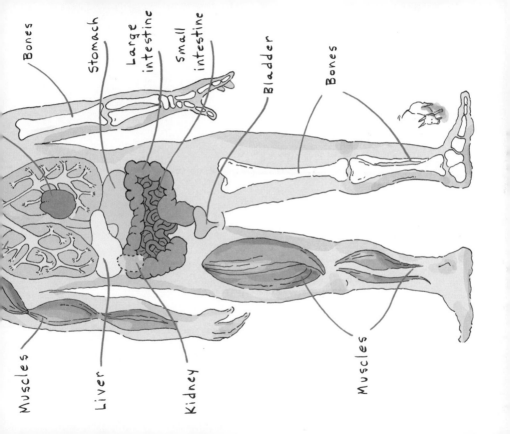

See It, Do It!

The friends dash off to the community centre to see what Coach Penny is planning. And — surprise! — it's a real national team swimmer at practice! The kids watch as she does deep breathing exercises before she dives in the pool. Coach explains that deep breathing has a calming effect on the body. If the five friends do this before their races tomorrow, it will help them focus and give them energy.

If you imagine winning a race or reaching a goal, it can often help you do it. This is called visualization.

It's the Big Day!

The next day at the swim meet, everybody is feeling great. Even Nick's shoulder feels better.

The team's hard work has paid off. Look at the swimmers go!

Sally is happy because she swam her personal best.

Words to Know

being active: to keep a body moving — helping the heart, lungs and muscles to stay strong

coach: someone who instructs and trains. A swimming coach can help prepare swimmers for an upcoming meet.

deep breathing: the technique of taking deep breaths to reduce anxiety or stress. Taking deep, slow breaths can help an athlete to focus and stay calm.

fuel: a source of energy. Bodies need fuel — healthy food and water — to work their best.

germ: an organism so small it can't be seen without a microscope. Germs can cause disease and infection. Washing hands with soap and water can help stop germs from spreading.

personal best: the best time or score an athlete has ever achieved

sports equipment: items used in sports for safety or to improve performance. Many sports require equipment, like a helmet for bicycling or shin pads for soccer.

team huddle: when a team gathers together in a tight circle to plan, encourage or celebrate

visualization: the act of picturing yourself reaching a goal. In sports, it can help prepare an athlete to cross that finish line!

warm up: to gently stretch and work muscles to prepare the body before being active. This is a good way to help avoid injury.

ACTIVITIES

Let's Play!

Get outside with your friends and play for 60–90 minutes every day to help you feel great from head to toe!

Here are a few ideas:

Bear Walk
This is great for any age. Players walk around on all fours, hands and feet on the ground. See who can go the fastest — or growl the loudest!

Splash!
With chalk, draw two lines on the pavement to represent a river — vary the width so that sometimes it's almost touching and other times it's 1.2 m (4 ft.) apart (at most). Players take turns "jumping the river." Use the chalk to mark where you landed.

RAWWWR!

Helicopter

Helicopter is a skipping game everyone can play together. Hold one handle of a skipping rope and ask everyone to form a circle around you. Then, lay the rope on the ground and spin it in a circle. Each player jumps over the rope as it goes by. Remember to take turns spinning the rope!

Search and Find

There are many ways of staying healthy and active!
Look at the following examples. Can you find where
these images appear in the story? When you do, write
the page number on the line below each image.

_____   _____   _____

Maze

Help Ollie get to the pool so he can watch the Flying Sharks!

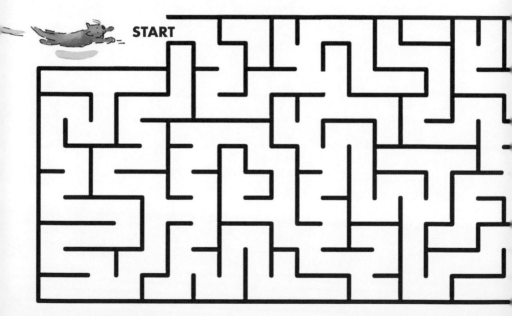

START

FINISH

Well-Being Challenge

Can you complete this ultimate well-being challenge?
Colour in the squares as you complete each task.
How many can you do? Try it with a friend!

Dance for 1 minute	Do 10 jumping jacks	Drink a glass of water
Eat a healthy snack	Do breathing exercises for 2 minutes	Do 5 frog jumps
Stand on one foot for 30 seconds	Have a quiet time	Stretch to touch your toes

Answers

Search and Find

Page 12

Page 20

Page 31

Page 14

Page 27

Page 16

Page 9

Page 12

Page 13

Answers

Maze

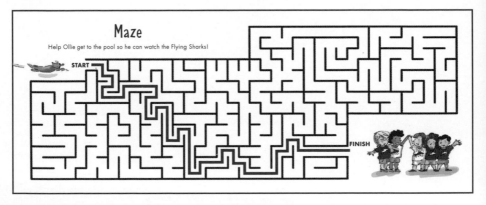